The Bible
Between
Fundamentalism
and Philosophy

HENRY P. HAMANN

The Bible Between Fundamentalism and Philosophy

AUGSBURG Publishing House • Minneapolis

Contents

Preface

The present book presents in slightly revised form three lectures delivered by the author at Valparaiso University from April 3-5, 1979. The lectures were sponsored by the Thomas F. Staley Foundation, "a private, non-profit organization, established to administer funds to further the evangelical witness of the Christian Church, and with a particular concern for college students." The actual topic was originally proposed by Dr. Norman E. Nagel, Dean of the Chapel of Valparaiso University. His choice of the topic was obviously not dictated by a purely personal interest in that subject but by actual experience of the needs of college students generally, which in turn is probably a pointer to a more general interest in the subject within the Christian church as a whole.

I have kept in this printed version of the lectures the personal forms of address appropriate to a lecture, where the lecturer seeks to win others to his or her special point of view.

The way to proceed in developing the subject seemed determined by the topic itself: to describe fundamentalism and point out how it poses a threat to the true understanding and use of the sacred Scriptures; to do precisely the same with respect to philosophy; and finally to describe and defend the safe, middle ground. The chapter headings of this book are, of course, the titles of the three lectures.

1

The Bible
and the Deviation
of Fundamentalism

Almost every writer who has to speak of *fundamentalism* complains about the inadequacy of the term and the difficulty involved in defining it. One example can be representative of many. J. I. Packer complains that the "word combines the vaguest conceptual meaning with the strongest emotional flavour"; that it "has long been a term of ecclesiastical abuse, a theological swearword"; and that as "its derogatory flavour grows stronger, it is used more and more widely and loosely as a general term of abuse, till it has lost all value as a meaningful description of anything." However, after pointing out the well-known historical origin of the term in the years following the publication of *The Fundamentals,* he in principle accepts the definition of the *Concise Oxford Dictionary* "when it defines 'Fundamentalism' as: 'maintenance, in opposition to modernism, of traditional orthodox beliefs, such as inerrancy of Scripture and literal acceptance of the creeds, as fundamentals of protestant Christianity.' " [1] Since the so-called *Deliverance* of the General Assembly of the Northern Presbyterian Church in 1910, five items appear regularly as "the fundamentals of faith and evangelical Christianity": the inspiration and infallibility of Scripture, the deity of Christ, his virgin birth and miracles, his substitutionary atonement for our sins, and his physical resurrection and personal return. It is, of course, the first of these which is our concern in this lecture.

It is of some moment, granted the general lack of precision which marks the use of the term *fundamentalism*, that I characterize much more closely what I myself understand by fundamentalism as far as the Sacred Scriptures are concerned. I have no doubt at all that very many people in the world would characterize my position, too, as 'fundamentalistic,' and that judgment would, in turn, disqualify me from delivering any lectures on the topic announced to you. So this lecture will take the following course. A series of eight broad features, followed by a number of characteristic fundamentalistic positions in detail, will—such is my hope—present you with a sharp profile of fundamentalism vis-à-vis the Scriptures. The rest of this lecture will endeavor to show the inadequacy of this view of Scripture on the basis of the Christian faith and of the heart of the Scriptures themselves.

The first of the eight broad features just referred to may be formulated as follows: Scripture is the first principle of the Christian faith; whatever is true in the Christian faith, is true only because the Scripture declares it to be so. Norman F. Furniss describes this position by means of the following enlightening comparison: "To the Fundamentalists, religious beliefs formed a pyramid, each tenet resting on the one below, with the infallible Bible as the broad foundation." [2] The position being described was put very bluntly and crassly in a letter to the editor which appeared in the January 8, 1979, issue of *Christian News:*

> The Jesus Christ Whom I know from Holy Scriptures, who was God, and IS God, never usurped the AUTHORITY OF THE HOLY SCRIPTURES to transfer that AUTHORITY TO HIMSELF. The JESUS CHRIST Whom I know from the Holy Scriptures, Who Himself WAS GOD, always subjected Himself to the AUTHORITY of "IT IS WRITTEN.". . . JESUS CHRIST did not get up on stage of this world and "AD LIB IT" . . . the HOLY SCRIPTURES were "SCRIPT" for Jesus' whole Life, Action and Words. . . . In their confusion [i.e., Paul Bretscher and John Holte Hagen as well as at least 1500 to 2000 pastors], they place the cart before the horse, that is, JESUS CHRIST before SCRIPTURE as the "WORD OF GOD," or, of [*sic*] PRIMAL AUTHORITY, instead of vice versa.

It is part of this way of thinking when fundamentalists make a doctrine of every statement or every fact, however inconsequential, that appears in the Scriptures. So the dimensions of the ark become a doctrine, as do the details of Absalom's rebellion or the number of years Aeneas was bedridden before Peter healed him, and thousands of other facts like these. With a view like this the

Bible becomes a law book with a whole host of definitive and authoritative sentences and paragraphs, none really and in principle more important than the next, except as may happen to judge from time to time.

The second of our delineating features is that of *inerrancy*. Since this word, too, is used in a number of different ways, despite its obvious formation, I am speaking of that inerrancy which is deduced from a human picture of the perfection of God. The argument is that since the Scriptures are inspired by God and since God knows everything and cannot possibly be mistaken, therefore the Scriptures must be inerrant. There is a direct line of argument from the perfection of God to this particular perfection of absolute accuracy and truthfulness in matters of fact. And so we find in a book on inerrancy published some 40 years ago the following sentence in a footnote: "He who says that Scripture has erred and can err is saying that God has erred and can err." [3]

It is but a logical extension of the characteristic just examined when fundamentalists are concerned not only to rebut every imputation of error in the Scriptures but also insist that this is a necessary corollary of the teaching of inerrancy. Thus Clark H. Pinnock writes in his well-argued and well-written book, *Biblical Revelation—The Foundation of Christian Theology:*

> It must be stressed, however, that unless Evangelicals seek to clear the Scripture from such reproach [i.e., "highly visible contradictions in the parallel accounts of Samuel, Kings and Chronicles"], their position is meaningless, for it would imply that belief in

infallibility would not be affected by errors in Scripture.... The difficulties, if we are to contend they are apparent and not real, must be grappled with seriously ... we must contest the notion that we have no responsibility to vindicate Scripture in a study of the phenomena themselves. A hypothesis which is compatible with anything and everything means nothing. The difficulties in Scripture *matter* to Evangelicals, and it is our duty to cope with them.[4]

And so books are written with the deliberate intention of refuting the charges that the Bible contains errors for the purpose of bolstering the faith of troubled Christians. My own late and deeply loved mentor in graduate school at Concordia Seminary, St. Louis, Dr. William Arndt, wrote two such books. Archaeological discoveries are carefully combed for evidence supporting the historical references of the biblical writers. The position taken on inerrancy (God cannot lie, therefore his book cannot lie; God cannot make a mistake, therefore his book cannot make a mistake) demands this laborious activity, especially when the position is linked with a fourth characteristic.

The fourth characteristic I shall describe is an exaggerated—a highly exaggerated—judgment as to the consequences of error in the Scriptures. A great number of witnesses could be assembled here agreeing with the statement I heard very often when I was a theological student in Adelaide: "If there is one error in the Bible, then we can be sure of nothing in it." Theodore Engelder quotes all manner of writers who make the same or a very similar claim, writers Christian and non-Christian. So H. L. Mencken: "If the Bible is true, then it is true from cover to cover." The liberal D. Schenkel: "If error is admitted at one point it is admissible at all points." The scoffer Paine: "If Matthew and Luke cannot be believed in their account of Christ's natural genealogy, how are we to believe them when they tell us He was the Son of God?" C. F. W. Walther: "When it is asserted that erroneous human material is mixed in with the divine content of the Holy Scriptures, then not only that portion but the whole of the Sacred Scriptures are rendered wobbly and shaky." [5] This approaches, but of course is not the same as, the Latin tag: *Falsus in uno, falsus in omnibus* ("In error at one point, in error at all points."). I am not now engaging in criticism of individual arguments, but I should like to point out that we treat no other book like this. A proven mistake in a scholarly work does not at all make us distrustful of the rest of it. Only if a book has repeated errors and mistakes do we finally conclude that the work is of no real use. We don't have to doubt the central thesis of a book just because of some inconsequential error way out on the periphery. The fundamentalist cast of mind makes the position of its adherents unnecessarily difficult.

A fifth characteristic of fundamentalism and the use of the Bible is a certain hesitancy to adopt, or on occasion even to consider, figurative interpretations; or, to put it positively, there is in fundamentalism a literalistic bent. One can see the reason for this. One of the oldest dodges in religious apologetics is the recourse to the symbolical and the figurative. Where statements cause a thinking inquirer offense—as in the anthropomorphic descriptions of gods and goddesses in Homer's Iliad and Odyssey—apologists are quick to counter: "That's only the apparent meaning. You don't see the deeper underlying meaning of the writer." So difficulties are wafted away in symbolism and allegory. Fundamentalists as I am describing them will not permit you to look on Genesis 1-3 as *in any way* figurative. Similarly, some would refuse even to examine the case for a fictitious, parabolic book of Jonah because of the reference to the book by Jesus in Matthew 12:

> An evil and adulterous generation seeks for a sign; but no sign shall be given to it except the sign of the prophet Jonah. For as Jonah was three days and three nights in the belly of the whale, so will the Son of man be three days and three nights in the heart of the earth. The men of Nineveh will arise at the judgment with this generation and condemn it; for they repented at the preaching of Jonah, and behold, something greater than Jonah is here (vv. 39-41).

Similarly, the narrative in the Book of Job, if not the lengthy dialogs, would be insisted on as historical because of the casual reference to Job in James 5:11. That we might have in these instances allusions to well-known works of literature, like those which we frequently find in our reading and which we often make ourselves, is regularly disallowed. An official statement advances a rather incautiously worded principle by which to determine literal and figurative sections of the Bible:

> This means that every statement of Scripture must be understood in its native sense, according to grammar, context, and linguistic usage of the time. Where Scripture speaks

historically, as for example in Gen. 1-3, it must be understood as speaking of literal, historical facts. Where Scripture speaks symbolically, metaphorically, or metonymically, as for example in Rev. 20, it must be interpreted on these its own terms.[6]

Recently I experienced a sixth feature of a fundamentalistic approach to the Bible in a review of a slight volume of mine on *New Testament Criticism*. I was faulted by the reviewer for confining myself to purely rational and historical argumentation in my discussions of the various forms of criticism met with in New Testament scholars. I did this chiefly for two reasons: first, in discussion with men and women who do not accept your faith presuppositions you have to argue, if you argue at all, without such presuppositions; and second, such presuppositions are in any case extraneous when discussing the actual form of the New Testament and the history behind it. As a historical collection of writings, it has to be treated wholly from a historical point of view. One can't determine whether a certain sentence, say the word of Jesus on the cross, "Father, forgive them; for they know not what they do!" was part of the author's original text by reference to faith, feelings, intuition, or any other nonrational factor, but only by the principles of textual criticism, both internal and external. Fundamentalists, in other words, are so concerned about the divine side of the Scriptures that they do not really take the human side seriously. The Bible is said to be different from other books not only by virtue of its inspiration, but its inspiration somehow removes it from history as well.

The seventh characteristic of fundamentalism is that there must be a direct and matching correspondence between Old Testament prophecy and New Testament fulfillment. This means not only that Old Testament prophecies are directly fulfilled, but that New Testament quotations of Old Testament passages must be in basic verbal agreement. There is for instance a prophecy spoken by Nathan to David promising him a special son. In the RSV the prophecy reads as follows:

> When your days are fulfilled and you lie down with your fathers, I will raise up your offspring after you, who shall come forth from your body, and I will establish his kingdom. He shall build a house for my name, and I will establish the throne of his kingdom for ever. I will be his father, and he shall be my son. ... I will not take my steadfast love from him, as I took it from Saul, whom I put away from before you. And your house and your kingdom shall be made sure for ever before me; your throne shall be established for ever (2 Sam. 7:12-16).

This prophecy is quoted in Heb. 1:5 and applied to Jesus, the Son of God. Direct fulfillment means that at the time of the prophecy both God and the prophet had in mind its fulfillment in Jesus of Nazareth, and that this was the intent of the prophecy, its meaning and purpose from the moment of its utterance. Interpreters and scholars on the whole would rather argue that the prophecy was fulfilled *directly* in David's son, Solomon, and only *indirectly* in Jesus as a later descendant (of whom indeed Solomon may be regarded as a type).

The demand for basic verbal agreement in Old

Testament prophecies and their quotation in the New Testament may be well illustrated from a comparison between the *RSV* and *An American Translation* (Beck's Bible). Beck writes in his preface:

> God gave us in our Bible a historical structure that holds up before us in the Old Testament the promised Saviour and in the New the Saviour who has come.... The RSV undermines this plan of salvation by cutting down the prophecies of the coming Saviour in the Old Testament and the important truths about Christ in the New Testament. In this way it forfeits every privilege of being the Bible of the Christian Church.

> My translation ... gives the Church every Old Testament promise of the Saviour and every doctrine given in the text. For this reason my translation deserves a place, not merely as a help, but at the centre of the Christian Church so that every sinner will hear the richest doctrinal voice of his God giving Christ to him and every Christian truth God wants us to have.[7]

Now let us see what Beck has done and compare that with the RSV. Take Heb. 1:7. Beck has: "He makes his angels winds and his servants fiery flames" (that is what the Greek of Heb. 1:7 actually says). Now the passage quoted here is Ps. 104:4, which Beck translates as follows: "You make Your angels winds and Your servants flames of fire." In doing this he preserves a perfect match between fulfillment and prophecy. The RSV translations of the two passages are as follows: "Who makes his angels winds and his servants flames of fire" (Hebrews; this is like Beck). However, Psalm 104 runs, "who makest the winds thy messengers, fire and flame thy ministers." This is what the Old Testament says, and this is what makes sense as well. I will return to this particular matter, the relation between prophecy and fulfillment, in a slightly different connection.

The final characteristic I want to mention refers to a certain attitude or cast of mind which seems to be true of many fundamentalists. It certainly is not true of all, and I want that to be quite clearly understood. But a certain antiintellectualism shows up quite regularly. Packer complains about this in his book and says,

> American Fundamentalism did not in every respect adorn its doctrine. We honour the original Fundamentalists for their zeal to defend and spread their evangelical faith, but at a generation's distance from them we can see serious limitations in the witness which they made. They were, by and large, outclassed by their opponents in learning and ability. . . . Partly in self-defence, the movement developed pronounced anti-intellectual bias; it grew distrustful of scholarship, sceptical as to the value of reasoning in matters of religion and truculent in its attitude towards the argument of its opponents. Something less than intellectual integrity appeared in its readiness to support good cause with a bad argument. Its apologetics were makeshift, piecemeal and often unprincipled and unsound.

This characterization matches some of my experiences exactly. Many people who have an inclination toward fundamentalism just cannot see any point of view but their own. A simple reference to a text and the claim that it is the Word of God— that's all that is regarded as necessary. To suggest that Mark's style is somewhat cumbersome and lacking a little of the beauty of Plato, this is to them besmirching the fair name of God's book. At the same time we must never forget that there are many people classed as fundamentalists in their attitude to the Bible who are not like this at all, whose earnestness and intellectual caliber can be disregarded only at one's own peril.

I should like to complete my description of fundamentalism with a more detailed presentation of a number of what may be called classical cases. The first concerns Genesis 1 and the days of creation. The Lutheran Church of Australia in 1972 adopted a doctrinal statement on Genesis 1–3 which included the following assertion:

> In keeping with the statement made earlier it is not the intention of this section ('Literary-Historical Aspects and Sources') to assert dogmatically what interpretation of these difficult chapters or what approach to an interpretation is alone possible within the Church. And the Theses of Agreement in Section 1 show how differences of interpretation must be distinguished from church divisive differences over doctrine.

A footnote makes the specific reference: "The proper understanding of the seven days of Genesis 1, which has been much discussed over the years, is involved here." The fundamentalism I am describing will not accept such a refusal to come down in favor of a particular interpretation. It is rather asserted that the words of the chapters are clear, that they must be taken in their native sense, that there is nothing of a figurative way of speaking indicated by the text, that the text therefore establishes a doctrine of a six-day creation, in spite of the fact that the church *in toto* throughout the centuries, and the Lutheran Confessions as well, has not made any confessional statement on this point. Reference to the highly artificial arrangement of the material, the close correspondence between the first three days of creation and the next three, the schematic arrangement of things created leading to a climax in the creation of human beings, limitation of the things created to what people can see and notice with the unaided eye, and the evident marks of an undeveloped science—all these observations leave the committed six-day creationist unmoved. The argument is always that a text must be understood literally unless clear indication of figurative intent is to be found. Refusal to accept the literalistic interpretation is seen as a sign of unbelief or incipient unbelief and rebellion against the Word of God. One sometimes even hears statements like, "If you can treat these words as nonliteral in intent, why not do the same with the descriptions of the crucifixion, death, and resurrection of Jesus Christ?"

My second example is the translation of one word in Isa. 7:14, a Hebrew word, *ha almah.* Must this be translated as "a virgin," or will "a young woman" do? The heart of the debate here is that when the New Testament refers to this passage in connection with the birth of Jesus (Matt. 1:23), it uses the Greek word for "virgin." The Hebrew *ha almah,* however, is not the normal word for "virgin." It is used only four times in the Old Testament, and in each case a virgin *might* be involved, but not necessarily so. The word, according to Old Testament lexicographers, describes a young woman capable of bearing children. The argument for the translation "virgin" is not based on the meaning in the passage concerned, nor in the other three passages where the word is used, but on the dogmatic construction as to the relation between prophecy and fulfillment which I referred to earlier. According to this view, where any Old Testament prophecy is quoted as fulfilled in the New Testament, there the exegete is spared all further trouble in understanding the Old Testament passage; the meaning—even of individual words—is determined by the New Testament reference. But this particular view of prophecy and fulfillment is not necessary in order to preserve the inspiration and authority of both the Old and New Testaments. The two Testaments are not the same, and prophecy is not fulfillment. The fulfillment adds a precision which the prophecy merely makes possible. Until the actual coming of Jesus Christ and the completion of his work with the sending of the Holy Spirit and his return to his Father, no one knew just how the Old Testament prophecies of God's salvation for all would be fulfilled. No one, taking the whole of the Old Testament into purview, could have forecast the incarnation, passion, and resurrection of Jesus Christ. But the prophecy was such that this way of fulfillment was possible. Once the fulfillment was there, then the intention of the Old Testament prophecy in the mind of God became clear, and there is now no other way in which a Christian believer can understand the intent of the prophecy. But the stage of prophecy is one thing and the stage of fulfillment another. "Young woman" is a proper translation for *almah* at the prophetic stage; it leaves the possibility open that Immanuel's mother will be a virgin. "Virgin" must be the translation of *parthenos* at the time of fulfillment, though it was anticipated already in the Greek version of Isa. 7:14, found in the Septuagint.

I wrote in this strain some years ago in reviewing Beck's *An American Translation* and soon learned that you just do not suggest any other translation but "virgin" in Isa. 7:14 if you want to be regarded as a "conservative" theologian. The rigidity and passionate feeling with which "virgin" is insisted on in Isa. 7:14 reveal as clearly as anything can the true nature of fundamentalism. All the characteristics of fundamentalism that have been enumerated seem to come to a focus at this point.

The most serious problem with the fundamentalistic attitude to the Bible is that it upsets the proper relation between Jesus Christ and the Spirit, or between the so-called material principle of the Reformation (that we are justified and saved by grace alone, without the deeds of the law, for Christ's sake through faith) and the formal principle (the prophetic and apostolic writings of the Old and New Testaments are the only rule and norm according to which all doctrines and teachers alike must be appraised and judged). In the Nicene Creed we confess that the Holy Spirit is "the Lord, the giver of life, who proceeds from the Father and the Son. . . . He has spoken through the prophets" (ICET). Fundamentalism reverses this relation of Son and Spirit, and its view of the Bible as that book which the Spirit inspired results in the Son proceeding from the Spirit.

There can be no doubt that in thinking of the Christian faith and the relation of God to it we must think in terms of the following order: Father, Son, Spirit. We have a key passage in 2 Cor. 5:18-20:

> All this is from God, who through Christ reconciled us to himself and gave us the ministry of reconciliation; that is, Christ was in God reconciling the world to himself, not counting their trespasses against them, and entrusting to us the message of reconciliation. So we are ambassadors for Christ, God making his appeal, through us. We beseech you on behalf of Christ, be reconciled to God.

First is the act of redemption and reconciliation, set in motion by God the Father and carried out by his Son, and then the message, the ministry of this great act of God in Christ. This ministry, as is hinted at in the text, is one in which the Holy Spirit is active. The phrase "making his appeal" is a reference to the Holy Spirit, for the Greek verb involved has the same root as the word translated as "Counselor" in the gospel of John. The Spirit bears witness to the act of God in Christ; this is his task; he accompanies every speaking of that message, both oral and written. The Spirit's work, his whole work, is this ministry of witnessing to Christ. So he proceeds from the Son, and has no independent task of his own. This view of the Spirit comes out even more forcefully in a number of passages in the Farewell Discourses of Jesus in John 14–17:

These things I have spoken to you, while I am still with you. But the Counselor, the Holy Spirit, whom the Father will send in my name, he will teach you all things, and bring to your remembrance all that I have said to you (14:25-26).

But when the Counselor comes, whom I shall send to you from the Father, even the Spirit of truth, who proceeds from the Father, he will bear witness to me; and you also are witnesses, because you have been with me from the beginning (15:26-27. Note how close the meaning of the last verse is to 2 Cor. 5:20. The witness of the apostles and the witness of the spirit become one).

I have yet many things to say to you, but you cannot bear them now. When the Spirit of truth comes, he will guide you into all the truth; for he will not speak on his own authority, but whatever he hears he will speak, and he will declare to you the things that are to come. He will glorify me, for he will take what is mine and declare it to you. All that the Father has is mine; therefore I said that he will take what is mine and declare it to you (16:12-15).

The Spirit is wholly devoted to witnessing to the Son. This is true also of the Scriptures which he inspired. The true doctrine of the Bible is part of the doctrine of the Holy Spirit. Wherever there is witness to Christ, either oral or written, there the Spirit is at work: in apostles, prophets, writers of the biblical books, preachers of the gospel, teachers of the Word. But all serve Christ. He is first and foremost, preeminent. Because of him, Scripture is Holy Scripture. Fundamentalism turns this around, as in the letter quoted earlier: "... they place the cart before the horse, that is, JESUS CHRIST before SCRIPTURE as the 'WORD OF GOD', or, of PRIMAL AUTHORITY, instead of vice versa." The *filioque* clause in the Nicene Creed ("... and the Son") shows that the writer of the letter is wrong. If there is to be an order, it must be Christ—Spirit, Christ—Scripture. A well-known children's hymn goes, "Jesus loves me this I know, for the Bible tells me so." Here much depends on the meaning of the word "know." It may stand if it means strict knowledge, but not if the implication is, "Jesus loves me, this is so, for the Bible tells me so."

First the Christ, then the Spirit. First the event, then the message. This is the case even if we think only in terms of the Old Testament. The Old Testament is true finally only in view of its New Testament fulfillment. Without the New Testament fulfillment—"The time is fulfilled, and the kingdom of God is at hand" (Mark 1:15)—the Old Testament is a Jewish book and not part of the Christian Bible. In retrospect, we can see that the Old Testament is fulfilled in the Christ. In prospect, looking forward from the point of view of the Old Testament saints, any number of fulfillments were in theory possible. Matthew 26:54 causes no difficulty here: "But how then should the Scriptures be fulfilled, that it must be so?" Even the Old Testament is not antecedent to the mind of God. The Scripture must be fulfilled because God's purpose must be fulfilled. Sacred Scripture is not an independent, original authority for itself, apart from him of whom it treats and the Father whose Son he is.

Sometimes revelation through deeds and revelation through words are seen as opposed to one another. Revelation is held to be (at least primarily) what God has done, not what he has said. But deeds and words belong together in God's revelation. God's revelation is God speaking. If he had not spoken, no one would know that he had acted. But it is also true that if there were no deeds there would be nothing to talk about. Fundamentalism in effect makes deeds secondary, and treats the Christian faith, which is rooted in history and the act of God at work in Jesus of Nazareth, as if we had to do with a collection of eternal truths, all set down in the Bible to be found, acknowledged as true, and taken to heart.

None of the Creeds include a statement on the Scriptures as part of their statement of faith. I believe in God the Father, in his Son, in the Holy Spirit, and in all the matters connected with this Trinity, but I do not believe in the Bible. My relation to the Bible is different from my relation to the salvation to which it bears witness. With its witness to Christ the function of the Bible comes to its proper conclusion. What is secondary and what is primary can be clearly seen at this point.

The late Gabriel Hebert was a shining light in the theological world of Adelaide in his day. He wrote as follows in the "Postscript" to his work *Fundamentalism and the Church:*

> The second matter that has impressed itself on me in the writing of this book is the manner in which the inadequacy of the doctrine of the Inerrancy of Scripture has demonstrated itself. It is too narrow to fit the facts: it cannot be carried through in the exegesis

of Scripture without resort to special pleading....[8]

Inerrancy *is* too narrow a way by which to describe the perfection of God in the Sacred Scriptures. Would an inerrant book actually establish the book to be divine? Even if it be granted that God could not be guilty of errors—and I don't deny this—there are other matters about books which, in my judgment, are at least as important as inerrancy, such as beauty of language and a satisfying of aesthetics in other ways. I should expect the books of the Bible, if they were in a human way to demonstrate divinity, to be more attractive as literature than any other books. But no one suggests that the New Testament in any way approaches the literary style of Sophocles, Homer, or Plato.

There *is* often a special pleading about the argumentation used to defend inerrancy. As one reads the arguments used to harmonize the various accounts of the cleansing of the temple, the variations in the same saying of Jesus in Matthew and Luke, or varying wordings of the superscription on the cross, one feels that the arguments become more and more threadbare and unbelievable.

Fundamentalism does not do justice to the actual phenomena of the biblical writings. But that actual situation is an essential part of a proper view of the Bible. A proper view of the Bible will endeavor to draw together the actual state of the biblical writings and the teaching concerning the Bible as set forth by our Lord and his apostles. The struggle for this adequate teaching still must go on, for a complete solution is still to be achieved. This can come only from the Lord of church and the Bible as a gift to humble and earnest meditation and prayer. In that prayer all Christians—fundamentalists and nonfundamentalists—should be anxious and only too pleased to join.

Chapter 1 footnotes

1. J. I. Packer, *'Fundamentalism' and the Word of God* (Eerdmans, 1958), p. 30.
2. Norman F. Furniss, *The Fundamentalist Controversy* (Yale, 1954), p. 15.
3. Theodore Engelder, *Scripture Cannot Be Broken* (Concordia, 1944), p. 74, note 46.
4. Clark H. Pinnock, *Biblical Revelation—The Foundation of Christian Theology* (Moody, 1971), pp. 195-196.
5. Engelder, pp. 76-77.
6. *Statement on Scripture,* adopted at the 1958 Synodical Conference Convention; also to be found in *Reports and Memorials* of the 44th Regular Convention of the Lutheran Church–Missouri Synod, pp. 485-486. The quotation is from Section IV, "The Interpretation of Scripture."
7. Packer, pp. 31-32.
8. Gabriel Hebert, *Fundamentalism and the Church* (Westminster, 1957), p. 148.

2

The Bible
and the Threat
of Philosophy

I have entitled my second lecture to you "The Bible and the Threat of Philosophy." You will recall that the first lecture was called "The Bible and the Deviation of Fundamentalism." The variation in the wording between "deviation" and "threat" is deliberate and points to certain personal convictions of mine as to the relative seriousness of the danger to a true biblical view posed by fundamentalism and philosophy. Philosophy is a far greater danger to Christian people, whose faith and life are determined by the Bible, than fundamentalism. It is far from being the case that the Bible is precisely mid-way between the extremes of fundamentalism on the one hand and philosophy on the other. Fundamentalism, for its part, does not do justice to the evidently human nature of the Bible in every one of its aspects, but philosophy sees *nothing but the human side.* Fundamentalism leaves the church with a book that is wholly divine, philosophy with one that is wholly human. The Word of God is lost wholly with philosophy, but it remains for the church with fundamentalism. Philosophy is destructive of the Christian faith *in toto*. This cannot be said of fundamentalism. In their evil effects they are not at all commensurable.

Philosophy in the present context will simply mean the setting up of human reason, of personal and subjective factors, in opposition to the claim to speak with divine authority which the Bible makes for itself. Philosophy in this sense takes many forms. But behind them all there is the single principle that the final authority for faith and life is the verdict of reason.

The philosophical attitude to Scripture has become crystallized in the so-called historical-critical method. The historical-critical method is not always described as clearly and sharply as it might be. On occasion we meet descriptions which may leave the reader in uncertainty as to what the historical-critical method really is. However, no one is helped by such a state of affairs. For understanding, we need clear ideas, sharp outlines, definitions that are as accurate as possible. R. P. C. Hanson provides such a clear description of the historical-critical method:

> Only a hundred years ago, most Christians of all traditions would have been content to describe the Bible as inerrant, infallible, and inspired equally in every part.... But in spite of shocked churchmen . . . the revolution moved inexorably on. It consisted in the simple but far-reaching discovery that the docu-

> ments of the Bible were *entirely conditioned
> by the circumstances of the period in which
> they were produced* (my italics)....It meant
> that the books of the Bible were henceforth
> open to being treated precisely as all other
> ancient documents are treated by historians
> of the ancient world. No sanctity, no peculiar
> authority, no special immunity to objective
> and unsparing investigation according to the
> most rigorous standards and methods of
> scholarship, could ever again be permitted to
> reserve the Bible from the curious eyes of
> scholars.[1]

The consequences which the historical-critical method as just described has had on the traditional biblical picture can be guessed by anyone with imagination, as they are well known by some in this audience. I intend at this point to present a brief survey of the changes in the attitude to the New Testament which application of the historical-critical method over the last two hundred years or so has brought about. There have been parallel changes of convictions concerning simply hundreds of questions in the Old Testament as well. However, I choose to restrict my survey to the New Testament material. In doing so I intend to proceed from the more superficial changes to the more central and crucial.

For centuries the church was satisfied with the form of the New Testament text which lies behind the King James Version, that is, the so-called Received Text. More recent editions of the Greek New Testament, which have made use of previously unknown manuscripts as well as modern text-critical principles, have been looked at with suspicion and sometimes been severely denounced.

Occasionally even today one runs across endeavors to defend the Received Text as the only legitimate text of the New Testament.

According to tradition, the writers of the Gospels are the four names we know so well. But modern scholars point out that the Gospels themselves are anonymous, and many are skeptical about the accuracy of the traditional designations. In fact it is regularly denied that the writers of the Gospels were the two apostles and the two apostolic men whom tradition names.

Historical criticism has also attacked traditional views concerning the authorship of many New Testament Letters. Here more than tradition is being attacked, for the actual claims of the Letters themselves are often denied. Some writers will grant only that the apostle Paul wrote Romans, 1 and 2 Corinthians, and Galatians. All the rest of the Pauline letters are therefore considered pseudonymous, as well as the remaining New Testament letters, such as those bearing the names of Peter, John, and James.

Critical and literary study of the Gospels has occupied scholars for years. The curious fact that three gospels are much alike and view the life of Jesus from much the same point of view (hence, *synoptic* gospels) while the fourth presents a very different picture of Jesus has led to especially intensive investigation. Many theories have appeared in order to account for the special character of John's gospel, theories concerning the sources of the materials, the identity and purpose of the writer, the situation of the church when it was written, the heretics the writer was opposing, and so on. The upshot of this study is that in spite of all the differences of opinion about other matters, scholars almost unanimously claim that John's gospel is not a reliable source for historical facts about the life and teaching of Jesus. The other gospels present what is called the "synoptic problem": how to account for both the close resemblances among them (general plan, order of events, and actual language in which these events are described) and at the same time the many differences as well. The commonly accepted solution (which, by the way, is being challenged more and more today) is that there are two main sources: Mark and a source labeled "Q" (for a German word meaning "source"). So Mark's gospel is regarded as the earliest gospel, one source of the other two synoptics. The common material in Matthew and Luke which is not found in Mark —and most of this is discourse material—is traced back to Q. Matthew and Luke have other material besides, which goes back to different sources.

Not all of these results can be designated as wrong or upsetting of biblical authority. Our knowledge of the language of the New Testament has been immeasurably increased and made more accurate by detailed investigation of the Greek of the New Testament period. It is plain from these studies that the Greek of the New Testament is not some heavenly Greek, Greek of the most perfect kind, nor a debased, bastard Greek, but simply the common Greek (*Koine*) of the period. Writers of the New Testament differ quite noticeably in their use of this Greek, but it is still the common Greek. The best medium for the spread of the gospel was the commonly-spoken language of that time. The detailed work involved in the study of early written texts has resulted in a situation where we can have great confidence in the basic text of our New Testament. The literary analysis of the texts, too, has brought us to better and better understanding of them, although we shall probably never understand them as well as those who first wrote and read them.

Many of the peripheral aspects of the historical-critical method have considerable value for a more perfect mastery of the sacred texts. This will continue to be true as long as these critical investigations deal with what is known: with manuscripts, with the actual texts of the various writings of the Bible, and with the actual texts of other writings which impinge here or there on biblical books. Strange, way-out, and radical theories concerning the biblical writings will be continually advanced, but the correction of these lies in the writings themselves. Sound reasoning soon relegates many of the wildest theories to limbo.

But the historical-critical method by no means stops with the kind of investigations I have so far mentioned. It criticizes the material of the various writings themselves, subjecting their contents to the bar of what is rational or possible. It compares the statements of one writer with those of another, and of one man with himself, pointing out differences, inconsistencies, and contradictions. To give an adequate picture of all this within the New Testament is too big a task. Accordingly, I shall confine myself mainly to the Gospels.

As mentioned earlier, John's gospel has long been regarded by the scholarly world as an unreliable historical source for the life of Jesus. In

John Jesus is too grand a figure, too overpowering in his divinity, really nonhuman in his effect on the reader. This effect, it was felt, quite convincingly disqualified the gospel as a reliable picture of Jesus. But it was not long before the same critical spirit raised doubts also as to the picture of Jesus that appears in the other gospels. Since Mark was regarded as the earliest, and a source for Matthew and Luke, it was natural to say that in Mark's gospel, if anywhere, we should find the truth about the life of Jesus. Wilhelm Wrede was to give a crushing blow to this view. He pointed out that one of the prominent features of Mark's gospel is the so-called messianic secret. In Mark Jesus regularly conceals any messianic claim and imposes silence on his disciples and others with respect to his own person. Wrede showed to his own satisfaction and that of many other scholars that this messianic secret was actually not a historical trait of Jesus at all, but a theological construction of the early church read back into the life of Christ and imposed on the gospel material. The church after Easter, which saw in Jesus the Lord and Christ, explained his nonacceptance by Israel before his death by the supposition that he had concealed his identity. So the historical reliability of Mark's gospel came under suspicion just like that of the other gospels.

Wrede's criticism was a foretaste of the situation which now holds sway in large parts of the scholarly world. Since about the end of the First World War, the interest in the history of the origins of the Christian faith has moved from the text of the Gospels as they stand to the period before they were written. Emphasis has been placed on the oral traditions about Jesus between the time he lived, preached, and died and the writing of the Gospels. The study devoted to a recovery of the origin and history of these traditions until they were fixed in writing is known as form criticism. A further development devoted to the theology of those who actually wrote the Gospels is known as redaction criticism. The net result of the work of these scholars (there are more radical and less radical among them) is that most of the material that we meet in the Gospels comes from the early Christian congregations, both Jewish and Hellenistic, and not from Jesus. The theology we find is the theology of the early Christians as they looked back on what happened from the vantage point of their belief that Jesus had risen and was now Christ and Lord. This faith in the risen Christ colored all their recollections and transformed their experience. They freely transferred to the earthly Jesus, both in word and deed, what they themselves thought and experienced under the influence of the risen Lord and his Spirit. The Gospels, then, leave us primarily with the thoughts, theology, and experiences of the early church. Jesus is the mysterious historical figure behind them who must be recovered by scholarly criticism.

It is interesting to see what the Jesus so recovered actually looks like, and to note the difference between that Jesus and the Jesus of the church's tradition. The traditional view sees full agreement between the Jesus of the Gospels and Jesus Christ as confessed in the Apostolic and Nicene Creeds. Jesus is the eternal Son of God who in a supernatural way was born as a true man, who by word and many miracles demonstrated his essential unity with God, and who at the end of his life was exalted to be the Lord of the church and of history by his death, resurrection, and ascension into heaven.

The Jesus of modern critical scholarship is as different from this picture as can possibly be imagined. Jesus was the son of Mary with an unknown father, who was probably born in Galilee about 5 B.C. He was probably at some time in his life a disciple of John the Baptist. His own public activity occurred a few years later, beginning a year or so before 30 A.D., in which year he most likely met his death. Hans Conzelmann declares that no more of the whole tradition of the Passion can be assured historically than that Jesus was condemned and that he was crucified. Some other aspects of the gospel story of Jesus may be historically accurate: that he was brought up in a rural area; that, unlike John the Baptist, he associated with men and women rather than cut himself off from them; that traveling from place to place preaching was, especially in Galilee, the characteristic form of his activity; that Capernaum was a center of his work; that at his death he had gathered around him a circle of followers (but the number 12 and the term *apostles* came later); that his teaching led him into conflict with scribes and Pharisees; that he traveled finally to Judea and Jerusalem and met his end in conflict with the Jewish hierarchy and the Roman authorities.

It is regularly held that the Gospels are not primarily interested in a history of Jesus, that they are anything but historical accounts or biographies. The following quotation from Günther Bornkamm is representative:

> Admittedly the synoptic Gospels themselves are not simply historical sources which the historian, enquiring after Jesus of Nazareth as a figure of the past, could use without examination and criticism... they unite to a remarkable degree both record of Jesus Christ and witness to him, testimony of the Church's faith in him and narration of his history.... We possess no single word of Jesus and no single story of Jesus, no matter how incontestably genuine they may be, which do not contain at the same time the confession of the believing congregation or at least are embedded therein. This makes the search after the bare facts of history difficult and to a large extent futile.[2]

It should be expressly noted that disagreements among modern critical scholars as to the amount of historical truth that can be determined are of no consequence in the long run. This is true for the scholars themselves, for it is held by them that faith is not dependent on the ups and downs of historical studies.

Historical critics are much happier and more sure when it comes to uncovering the teachings of Jesus. Rank-and-file Christians are not, however. For here, over the years, scholars have less and less to say. Accounts of Jesus' teaching become progressively shorter as the acids of criticism are applied to his transmitted words. All the titles of eminence are denied as having been claimed by Jesus: Messiah, Son of God, Son of Man, and the rest. "As far as we can see Jesus never used of himself any of the christological terms of glory found in the synoptic writers. Therefore it is impossible to reconstruct the self-consciousness of Jesus from these titles of eminence." [3] All that can be claimed about him in relation to his estimate of himself is that he understood himself and his work as the sign of the imminent kingdom of God. For the rest he called people to repentance, preached the coming of the kingdom, and enunciated a number of high ethical principles as God's will.

Enough has been said of the change that has been produced in the picture of Jesus by philosophy to warrant asking whether Jesus is still important for the Christian faith at all, whether there is any real connection between the Jesus of criticism and the Christ of the church's confession. But rather than pursue that question I will round off the whole picture I am painting by showing in the case of two famous scholars what sort of Christian faith (Christian gospel if you like) remains or is produced or is constructed once historical criticism has been consistently applied to the sources of the Christian faith, the Sacred Scriptures.

At the turn of the century tremendous excitement in the Christian world was occasioned by a small book written by Adolf von Harnack. The German version (*Das Wesen des Christentums* or "The Essence of Christianity") was translated into English under the title *What Is Christianity?* The public lectures underlying this work were originally delivered at the University of Berlin in the winter semester of 1899/1900. They made their first appearance in book form in 1900. By 1927 the book had been through 14 printings and had been translated into many languages. Although it exerted a tremendous influence on budding theologians and other educated people, it is now rarely read, even by theological students. However, many ministers are still under the influence of some of the ideas Harnack first enunciated in that book, and Harnack's view of Christianity is a good illustration of the point I am now making.

In his study of what Christianity really is, Harnack declared that he would "employ the methods of historical science and the experience of life gained by studying the actual course of history" as the proper means by which to arrive at the answer.[4] His answer was engagingly uncomplicated. "The Christian religion is something simple and sublime," he declared. "It means one thing and one thing only: eternal life in the midst of time, by the strength and under the eyes of God."[5] Or more completely:

> If, however, we take a general view of Jesus' teaching, we shall see that it may be grouped under three heads. They are each of such a nature as to contain the whole, and hence it can be exhibited in its entirety under any one of them.
> *Firstly, the kingdom of God and its coming.*
> *Secondly, God the Father and the infinite value of the human soul.*
> *Thirdly, the higher righteousness and the commandment of love.*[6]

As for the first of these three phrases, the kingdom is simply "God himself in his power," and he comes to the individual, "by entering into his soul and laying hold of it." It is a question "of God and the soul, the soul and its God. . . . Everything that

is external and merely future is abandoned: it is
the individual, not the nation or the state, which is
redeemed." [7] The kingdom is

> something supernatural, a gift from above . . .
> it is a purely religious blessing, the inner link
> with the living God . . . it is the most impor-
> tant experience that a man can have, that on
> which everything else depends; it permeates
> and dominates his whole existence, because
> sin is forgiven and misery banished.[8]

The second way of putting Christ's message—
God the Father and the infinite value of the human
soul—Harnack believes to be the most congenial
to the modern way of thinking.

> In the combination of these ideas—God the
> Father, Providence, the position as God's chil-
> dren, the infinite value of the human soul—the
> whole gospel is expressed. But we must recog-
> nize what a paradox it all is; nay, that the
> paradox of religion here for the first time
> finds its full expression . . . Either that is non-
> sense, or else it is the utmost development of
> which religion is capable.[9]

The whole of the gospel can also be embraced
under the idea of "the higher righteousness and
the commandment of love." [10] Harnack lists four
particular features of this higher righteousness:
Jesus severed the connection existing in his day
between ethics and the external forms of religious
worship and technical observance; in all questions
of morality Jesus went straight to the root, to the
disposition and the intention; what he thus freed
from its connection with self-seeking and ritual
elements, and recognized as the moral principle,

he reduced to *one* root and to *one* motive—love; and finally he combined religion and morality by making love and humility one.[11]

We turn from this great representative of what is known as liberal theology to the master of demythologization, Rudolf Bultmann. During the last world war there appeared an essay of his which proved as provocative as the work of Harnack. It was entitled *New Testament and Mythology* and had the subtitle "The Mythological Element in the Message of the New Testament and the Problem of its Re-interpretation."[12] One of the roots of the essay was the laudable intent to divest the Christian message of every aspect which might wrongly give offense to modern people so that they might be confronted with the true message of the Gospel and the true offense, which alone could bring them to the point of that decision upon which true life depends. The other roots were the conviction that the New Testament gospel is presented throughout in mythological dress, and can be best expressed today in terms of the existentialist philosophy of Martin Heidegger.

That the New Testament could become important for modern people only through demythologization becomes clear from the following brief summary of Bultmann's view concerning the New Testament as it stands:

> It is no longer possible for anyone seriously to hold the New Testament view of the world. . . . We no longer believe in the three-storied universe. . . . The only honest way of reciting the creeds is to strip the mythological framework from the truth they enshrine—that is, assuming that they contain any truth at all . . . we

> can no longer believe in spirits, whether good
> or evil . . . The miracles of the New Testa-
> ment have ceased to be miraculous . . . The
> mythical eschatology is untenable for the sim-
> ple reason that the parousia of Christ never
> took place as the New Testament expected . . .
> Man is essentially a unity. He bears the sole
> responsibility for his own feeling, thinking,
> and willing . . . He finds what the New Testa-
> ment has to say about the "Spirit" and the
> sacraments utterly strange and incomprehen-
> sible. Biological man cannot see how a super-
> natural entity like the pneuma can penetrate
> within the close texture of his natural powers
> and set to work within him . . . It is impos-
> sible to revive an obsolete view of the world
> by a mere fiat, and certainly not a mythical
> view. For all our thinking today is shaped for
> good or for ill by modern science.[13]

If this criticism is not radical enough for you, see
how Bultmann finished his description of the problem.

> And as for the pre-existence of Christ, with
> its corollary of man's translation into a celes-
> tial realm of light, and the clothing of the
> human personality in heavenly robes and a
> spiritual body—all this is not only irrational
> but utterly meaningless.[14]

The New Testament as it stands, then, has to be
seen as presenting truth in mythological form. But
what truth? After reviewing a number of attempts to get behind the myth to the truth, in-
cluding the path of Harnack, Bultmann declared
that only the existentialist interpretation is true
and fitting. He holds that the New Testament of-
fers human beings an understanding of them-

selves which challenges them to a genuine existential decision, that is, to live "authentically." Until they have come to faith, human beings lead an "unauthentic" life, a life determined by the attempt to find security in earthly, temporal things. "The authentic life, on the other hand, is a life based on unseen, intangible realities. Such a life means the abandonment of all self-contrived security." [15] This is said to be an unmythological interpretation of the Christian understanding of being or existence.

Bultmann is at pains to show how the Christian understanding of being differs from that of existential philosophy. He says:

> It might well appear possible to have a Christian understanding of Being without Christ, as though what we had in the New Testament was the first discovery and the more or less clear expression, in the guise of mythology, of an understanding which is at bottom man's natural understanding of his Being, as it has been given clear expression in modern existentialist philosophy.[16]

The difference between them, he holds, is that a human being is "capable of knowing that his authentic life consists in self-commitment (this is what philosophy can point out), but man is incapable of realizing it, because however hard he tries he still remains what he is, self-assertive man. So in practice authentic life becomes possible only when man is delivered from himself." This deliverance is what God has accomplished in Christ. "The New Testament speaks and knows of an act of God through which man becomes capable of self-commitment, capable of faith and love, of his authentic life." This act is the death and resurrection of Jesus. However, resurrection is not anything that actually happened to Jesus—he is as dead as a doornail. *"Faith in the resurrection is really the same as faith in the saving efficacy of the cross."* We must not think that anything special happened when Jesus was crucified, that any change in the relation between God and human beings took place. The real nub of the matter is in the preaching of cross and resurrection, or the saving power of the cross.[17]

> How do we come to believe in the cross as the cross of Christ and as the eschatological event *par excellence*? How do we come to believe in the saving efficacy of the cross? There is only one answer. This is the way in which the cross is proclaimed. It is always proclaimed together with the resurrection. Christ meets us in the preaching as one crucified and risen. He meets us in the word of preaching and nowhere else . . . The word of preaching confronts us as the word of God. It is not for us to question its credentials. It is we who are questioned, we who are asked whether we believe the word or reject it.[18]

In spite of the close resemblance between much of this and the traditional preaching of the Gospel, especially in its Lutheran dress, there is no real agreement at all. There is no object for the faith Bultmann speaks so much about. Faith is authentic existence, that is all, and instead of believing in Jesus, modern people are asked to believe like Jesus and live an authentic life as he did.

In the case of most Christians, the mere introduction to the results of philosophy's examination of the Bible and its teaching is enough to call forth a quite specific and distinct rejection of the entire enterprise. They know that the differences between the faith in which they were brought up and the faiths of Harnack and Bultmann are such that we are faced with separate religions, not with variations within Christianity. And they want nothing of the novelties which philosophy and the historical-critical method bring into being. "Lord, to whom shall we go?" they ask, and go on to declare, "You have the words of eternal life." If they were to go elsewhere, there would be no particular reason why they should take the path to the faith of Bultmann. Certainly I would find my way to an Epicurean rather than to Bultmann any day. "Eat, drink, and be merry, for tomorrow we die." This is existential enough. And Epicureanism is at least as likely to produce characters with whom we can get along for the brief space of this life as the complicated philosophy of Heidegger and Bultmann.

The two brands of Christianity produced by philosophy which we have just described should cause no real surprise. Results like these could have been predicted. I should like to point out why this is true.

First, as judge of biblical claims and teachings, philosophy effectively excludes the Bible as the source of Christian faith and life. Once human wisdom has been granted the right to be judge and arbiter in one instance, in one direction, no argument can be advanced why it should not be arbiter in each and every place. So philosophy displaces Scripture.

In addition, the Bible and human wisdom are inherently, fundamentally incompatible; they are irreconcilable opposites. St. Paul has written sharply and unforgettably about this in his first letter to the Corinthians.

> For the preaching of the cross is to them that perish, foolishness; but unto us which are saved, it is the power of God ... For after that in the wisdom of God the world by wisdom knew not God, it pleased God by the foolishness of preaching to save them that believe ... Howbeit we speak wisdom among them that are perfect: yet not the wisdom of this world, nor of the princes of this world that come to nought: But we speak the wisdom of God in a mystery, even the hidden wisdom, which God ordained before the world unto our glory; Which none of the princes of this world knew: for had they known it, they would not have crucified the Lord of glory. But as it is written, Eye hath not seen, nor ear heard, neither have entered into the heart of man, the things which God hath prepared for them that love him (1:18—2:9 KJV).

All Christians know that the apostle is speaking nothing but the truth here. They have experienced in their own hearts and souls and brains that the Christian gospel, the message of the Scriptures, and human wisdom come into continual conflict. Just think for a moment of various aspects of the faith. What sort of mathematics is the doctrine of the Trinity? How can Jesus of Nazareth be both God and man at one and the same time? What sort of man is left when the unlimited, eternal, almighty God dwells in him bodily? And how unjust of God to hold people guilty and responsible for their sin when they are sinful and corrupt by inheritance and birth! How monstrous a miscarriage of justice and all moral thinking for God to allow his son to suffer vicariously, the innocent for the guilty! And then to declare the vilest and foulest sinner right in his sight and forgive him freely, justifying the ungodly, condemning Jesus and acquitting Barabbas! What nonsense is this talk of regeneration, forgiveness of sins, life, and salvation for a squawking infant upon whose head some water is poured and to whom a few words are spoken? And in innumerable celebrations of Holy Communion over the centuries bread and wine have supposedly transmitted the body and blood of a dead criminal who is said to have been raised to a new and nondefinable spiritual life! On and on we could go. Unbelievers and critics of the Christian faith at times try to overwhelm believers with the incongruities, nonsensicalities, and irrationalities of their faith. They would do well to conserve their energy. Thinking believers know and have been tempted over and over again by far more difficulties than unbelievers can produce. For Christians know the faith from the inside; they are experts and connoisseurs in this matter, and critical unbelievers are rank amateurs by comparison.

So Scriptural teaching and philosophy are incompatible. They are, to use Luther's phrase from another connection, "more than contradictory." That being so, philosophy cannot be anything but a threat—a most serious threat—to the Bible and what the Bible is all about, namely the gospel of forgiveness, life, and salvation through and because of the merits, suffering, death, and resurrection of Jesus Christ. As critics and judges, human wisdom and philosophy will always be threats to the gospel. The nature of philosophy, on the one hand, and of God's revelation through Christ on the other, combine to produce this mutual incompatibility and antagonism.

Of course if one looks at the biblical material apart from its central concern, then there is a great deal there which human wisdom will find congenial. And on a quite different level, reason is absolutely necessary for understanding the Bible. I will say more about this in the next lecture. The Bible and philosophy, then, are not opposites in *every conceivable respect*, but they are opposites in the *most important respect*, in respect of that which is proposed as truth for human beings to accept in faith—the gospel of Jesus Christ. Here lies the threat of philosophy to the Christian faith and to Christian believers. Here the leaders of the church—its pastors and teachers—must be on the alert to warn against human wisdom and its baleful effects, and so preserve for the church and the world the Word and truth which alone can save both.

Chapter 2 footnotes

1. *The Pelican Guide to Modern Theology* (Penguin, 1970), vol. 3, p. 00.
2. Günther Bornkamm, *Jesus of Nazareth* (Harper and Row, 1960), p. 14.
3. Translated from H. Conzelmann and A. Lindemann, *Arbeitsbuch zum Neuen Testament* (J.C.B. Mohr, 1976), p. 372.

4. Adolf von Harnack, *What Is Christianity?* (Harper and Brothers, 1957), p. 6.

5. Harnack, p. 8.

6. Harnack, p. 51.

7. Harnack, p. 56.

8. Harnack, p. 60.

9. Harnack, p. 62.

10. Harnack, pp. 68-69.

11. Harnack, pp. 71-72.

12. Contained in *Kerygma and Myth—A Theological Debate,* ed. Hans Werner Bartsch, trans. Reginald H. Fuller (Harper and Row, 1961).

13. Bultmann, pp. 3-8.

14. Bultmann, p. 8.

15. Bultmann, p. 19.

16. Bultmann, p. 23.

17. The material here is a very short presentation of Bultmann's argument on pp. 22-41.

18. Bultmann, p. 41.

3

The Bible
and the Word
of God

So far in these lectures we have been concerned with erroneous ways of looking at and assessing the Bible, with movements away from a sound and appropriate view of it. The first was to the right, the second to the left. One movement is far more serious than the other. However, there is a more excellent way, which is the subject of this final lecture.

I shall begin with a theoretical statement, and the greater part of the lecture will be an exposition of that statement: *That the Bible is truly the Word of God cannot be given up without loss of the Christian faith.*

That the Bible, all of it, is the Word of God must be held together with the assertion that it is, all of it, the word of human beings. A certain analogy exists here between the Word of Scripture and the personal Word who is Jesus Christ. As Christ is

God and man indivisibly associated in one person, so the Word of Scripture is both human and divine in an indissoluble unity. Everything about the Bible shows its humanity: the origin and genesis of the individual writings; the collection of the various and very different compositions into one definitive library; the transmission of the text of the various writings down through the centuries; and the translations from the original languages.

That the Bible is the Word of God must be held without falling into the mistake of making the Bible and the Word of God identical, as if the two expressions were completely conterminous—*Bible* conveying the same connotation as *Word of God,* and *Word of God* precisely the same connotation as *Bible.* As a matter of fact, *Word of God* is a far wider term than *Bible. Bible* is included in *Word of God.*

Word of God is applied repeatedly to the oral human statements about God, to those made by the many prophets in the Old Testament and by the apostles and others in the New. All the words of the prophets were, first of all, oral proclamations and these oral proclamations were truly the Word of God. Only a portion of these oral proclamations finally found their way into written form, and some of the prophets did not commit any of their spoken words to writing. The same is true of the New Testament. St. Paul praised the Thessalonians in the following terms: "And we also thank God constantly for this, that when you received the word of God which you *heard* from us, you accepted it not as the word of men but as what it really is, the word of God" (1 Thess. 2:13; italics added). What was true of St. Paul was true of the other apostles of Jesus Christ. Paul's letters represent only a very small portion of all he spoke in his preaching, teaching, admonishing, and advising. Most of the words that he spoke as the Word of God are not recoverable. This is even more the case with the other apostles, of whose words we have next to nothing.

The Word of God must also be used to describe the oral words of Jesus Christ himself, just as he is the personal Word. Some of his words have been transmitted in the Gospels, perhaps all the important ones. But the nonrecorded words must far exceed these. The writer of John 21:25 pointed to this fact in his highly exaggerated statement, "But there are also many other things which Jesus did; were every one of them to be written, I suppose that the world itself could not contain the books that would be written." More of the Word of God that is not part of the Bible!

We can go even further and declare that all proclamation of the gospel down the years by successors of the apostles and their successors down to our own age is properly designated as the Word of God. This includes every form in which this proclamation has taken place: speaking, signing, painting, sculpture, and architecture. Ministers should have the conviction every time they preach that they are proclaiming the Word of God. The spoken word can be as much the Word of God as the written word. Some words of Luther in the *Smalcald Articles* are worth hearing in this connection:

> In these matters, which concern the external, spoken Word, we must hold firmly to the conviction that God gives no one his Spirit or

> grace except through or with the external
> Word which comes before. Thus we shall be
> protected from the enthusiasts—that is, from
> the spiritualists who boast that they possess
> the Spirit without and before the Word and
> who therefore judge, interpret, and twist the
> Scriptures or spoken Word according to their
> pleasure. Muenzer did this. . . . The papacy,
> too, is nothing but enthusiasm, for the pope
> boasts that "all laws are in the shrine of his
> heart," and he claims that whatever he de-
> cides and commands in his churches is spirit
> and law, even when it is above and contrary to
> the Scriptures or spoken Word.[1]

Occasionally one hears highly exaggerated statements to the effect that only the spoken Word is powerful, while the written Word is powerless and dead; that only when spoken does the Word come to life. To say this is to be insensitive to the nature of human language. I suppose that choice sections from the cantos of Milton's *Paradise Lost,* when declaimed or recited by a master reader or orator, woud have a greater and more gripping effect on the average hearer than the same passages read by him or her. It is also true that if read aloud by a poor reader they would be hopelessly ruined. But the passages retain their power to excite the imagination and arouse wonderment and admiration even when read silently. Similarly, the gospel is just as much the Word of God when read from the Bible as it is when it is spoken.

There is a unity about all these forms of the Word of God. I should like to let the late Dr. Hermann Sasse, a great scholar in many fields of theology and a personal friend for many years, speak on this point.

"The Word of the Lord will stand for ever." It belongs to the nature of God's Word in contrast to human words that it cannot perish. The Word of God in creation, each of these words, is living and powerful even today. The word spoken by God before there was a human ear to hear is identical with the word later recorded in writing. The word that came to a prophet in a definite hour of history remains and is identical with the word written in Scripture, as it is identical with the word read from Scripture and proclaimed in the sermon according to Luther's rule: *"Verbum Dei praedicatum est Verbum Dei"* ("The Word of God preached is the Word of God"). One must always keep in mind that the Word —or a particular word—exists in various forms: in the heart of God, going out of his mouth, coming to the prophet, heard by him, proclaimed by him, written in Scripture, read learned, remembered, translated, accompanying the dying soul—always the same powerful and living word.[2]

Granted the unity of the word of Scripture with all the other forms of the Word of God, the Scripture is still the Word of God in a special way which makes it characteristically different from the other forms. It is permanent, approachable, readily available, and as the permanent form of the word of the prophets, Jesus Christ, and the apostles, it is the source and authoritative norm of all preaching and teaching in the church of God. This definition needs some clarification.

The heart of the biblical revelation is the history of God's great acts for the salvation of human beings. Up to a point it is a recital of God's involvement in the course of history to bring about his saving plans and purposes. In the Old Testament special importance attaches to the deliverance of the people of Israel from Egypt, God's guidance of them through the desert, and his final settling of them in the land of Palestine. This great act of God is referred to repeatedly in subsequent literature, in the Psalms and the various prophetic writings. The whole event was kept alive by the Passover festival and the customs which grew up around it, right up to the time of the coming of Jesus Christ. In Christ a great, new, and final act of God for humankind was enacted. "In Christ God was reconciling the world to himself, not counting their trespasses against them, and entrusting to us the message of reconciliation" (2 Cor. 5:19). The incarnation, death, and resurrection of Jesus Christ dominate the New Testament writings as the Exodus does those of the Old. The whole situation is quite unlike other religions which have been fixed in writing, which have to do with the transmission of spiritual wisdom, teachings, and doctrines—all of which are claimed to be eternally true. Christianity and the religion of the people of God in the Old Testament are not like this at all, although there are, of course, these elements there as well. The Christian faith is based on and rooted in a history. Take that away, and there is nothing left in of the faith and in the Bible that you could not find elsewhere. This fact about the Christian faith has led some to see the revelation in the history itself, in God's acts themselves.

Such a view falls into a different error. As a matter of fact, there is nothing about the history itself, in either the Old or New Testaments, which is in any way obviously revelatory. There is nothing about the history of salvation as we see it in the Bible which by itself would demonstrate that in this particular history God acted in a special way for human beings, but not in all the rest of the mighty historical canvas involving many great nations, living, working, and dying over a period of 6000 years. Other nations have sprung from insignificant beginnings and within a few years attained a power and influence which Israel in the Old Testament never even began to approach. Other people besides Jesus of Nazareth have been unjustly crucified or condemned to other deaths just as cruel and inhuman. What is there about this death which is so special? What separates, from a purely historical perspective, Jesus from Socrates? Revelation, however, does not attach to God's deeds themselves or to the history in itself. Revelation occurs when God speaks to the deed. Revelation of God is the speaking of God. Word attached to the history—this is the decisive factor.

The Bible is the permanent record of God's speaking to these great acts of his. The spoken Word which reveals God's hand and activity in the historical events of the past, that Word is kept and preserved as the same Word by the Scriptures, the written Word of God. The spoken words of the prophets as they proclaimed the Word of God are no longer available to us. Neither are the spoken words of the apostle or of Jesus himself. Even the historical Jesus Christ, the person through whom God has spoken in a final, definitive way, is not directly approachable by us. The Word of the Scripture, in short, is the permanent "abstract" of the Word of God spoken in their day by the people of God of the Old and New Testaments: Moses, the prophets, psalmists, apostles, evangelists, and our Lord Jesus Christ himself. As such it is the original Word of God. No one can penetrate behind it to something still more original, still more basic and fundamental, still closer to its source, God himself. Neither liturgy, nor tradition, can take the place of the Scriptures as the original Word of God. Accordingly, although identifying the Bible and Word of God as conterminous fails to do justice to the many forms of the Word of God, the Bible is the Word of God in a very special sense. It is therefore also the source and norm of all teaching and preaching.

The last of the Lutheran confessional writings, the *Formula of Concord*, states the position of the Scriptures as the Word of God in the following terms:

> We believe, teach, and confess that the prophetic and apostolic writings of the Old and New Testaments are the only rule and norm according to which all doctrines and teachers alike must be appraised and judged. . . .
> Other writings of ancient and modern teachers, whatever their names, should not be put on a par with Holy Scripture. Every single one of them should be subordinated to the Scriptures and should be received in no other way and no further than as witnesses to the fashion in which the doctrine of the prophets and apostles were preserved in post-apostolic times.[3]

These words do not state, as they might be taken to do, that the words written and spoken by pastors and teachers of the church and others speaking as Christians are not truly the Word of God, but something less than Word of God. What the Formula is saying is that the Bible is the authoritative Word of God. It is the source and norm. Sermons, exhortations, essays, and other productions by men and women of the church are the Word of God only in so far as they are in keeping with the teaching of the Bible. For authority, true authority, we have to go beyond them to the Scriptures. All teachers and teachings in the church can be criticized and set right in a way that the Bible cannot be. It is possible that some great teacher can present a biblical truth more sharply and more incisively than the Bible itself does—for instance, Luther probably expresses the biblical view of human sin more profoundly than does the Bible itself. But his statements do not for that reason displace the biblical statements—they are rather to be assessed as the Word of God by the biblical norm.

In all this the Bible is the witness of the Spirit to Christ. As the Bible itself asserts in a number of places, we speak rightly of the Scriptures as inspired. Every true witness to Christ—by whomsoever given—is also the witness of his Spirit. Jesus himself unites the witness of his apostles and the witness of the Spirit in John 15:26-27, and this is insisted on also in other places, as in 2 Cor. 5:20. So also the written witness of the people of God which we have in the Bible is the witness of the Spirit. This inspiration extends over the whole of what is the Scriptures. Inspiration is verbal, for we think and speak in words. There is no other possible kind of inspiration of verbal material.

That the Bible is the Word of God in the way I have now outlined cannot be given up without loss of the Christian faith. Imagine the situation if the words of Jesus and the apostles had not been committed to writing. The oral transmission of these things down the years by word of mouth would by this time have transformed them beyond recognition. The Gospel of Thomas is only one indication of what we could expect. The apocryphal gospels show serious perversions of the nature and character of Christ Jesus in the popular imagination within a few centuries. Without the protection of a written Word of God, the imagination, whims, and vagaries of the human mind, together with its speculations, wishes, and desires would have left us with a multitude of conflicting words, sayings, assertions, and teachings through which no mind could penetrate to the original. Heaven knows, we have enough confusion as it is in theology. Not only common people but also trained theologians are hard-put to find their way through it all. Dr. Sasse had a fine comparison for such a state of affairs. He used to liken tradition where there is still a written Word to a balloon firmly anchored to the ground. It might be carried here and there by the wind, it might go through some violent gyrations, but it can't get too far away. The correction and stability offered by the Bible is always there. The case is far different with a balloon unattached and unanchored. There is absolutely no check to its movements. The winds carry it far away from the place where it left the ground, and there is no assurance that it will ever see the place again. So is tradition without a written Word of God.

The question is sure to be asked at this point, What is the difference between your position on the Bible as the Word of God and the position taken by fundamentalism? There is a difference, but it must first of all be granted that this position shares a number of convictions with fundamentalism. Both positions would maintain that the Bible is in all its parts the Word of God; that the Bible has unity; that it is the authoritative source and norm of faith and morals; that it is verbally inspired; that it calls for faith in certain propositions as well as faith in a person. But the differences between fundamentalism as I have described it and what I have just presented are there as well.

The first and most important difference, I should say, lies in the relation between all the incidental aspects and features of this library of books and the central Christian gospel. The tendency in fundamentalism is to see in all the many assertions many individual truths, all of which are valuable in themselves, all of them important, all of them the revealed Word of God, and (sometimes) all of them of more or less equal importance as the Word of God. The Bible becomes something like a codex of legal paragraphs, each of which must be upheld for fear of losing the whole. From the fundamentalistic point of view, for instance, it is impossible to prove a Seventh Day Adventist missionary wrong who insists on keeping the Sabbath and who refuses to allow his New Guinea converts to eat pork, in spite of the fact that pork is about the only animal protein a New Guinean villager is ever likely to eat. The regulation and the prohibition are there in the Old Testament, black on white, as clearly stated as possible. The view of the Bible presented here sees the whole Bible as related to its center, the gospel of Jesus Christ and God's work in him. "You search the Scriptures, because you think that in them you have eternal life; and it is they that bear witness to me" (John 5:39). True study of the Scriptures is study that never loses sight of the Christ of whom the Scriptures treat, and without whom they would have no particular value. With such a view of Scripture it is comparatively easy to argue the case of the Sabbath and pork.

Secondly, it is but an extension of the point of view just mentioned to see the gospel of Jesus Christ as a determining principle of Scriptural interpretation. This claim must be understood correctly. It does not suggest that the doctrine of justification by faith or the gospel is that from which all Christian teaching may be deduced. What it does say is that Scripture cannot teach anywhere what runs counter to its central teaching, the Gospel. It is a negative norm, if I may put it that way, not a positive norm. No one could deduce the sacraments of Baptism and the Lord's Supper from the doctrine of justification by faith, but it is also quite obvious that they are completely in harmony with that teaching. Both are derived from specific passages. On the other hand, the Gospel does indicate in various ways what the sacraments *cannot* be, and how they should *not* be regarded. So in many instances the gospel of Jesus Christ keeps an expositor from adopting some explanation of a certain passage which is plainly inconsistent with the gospel. The inspiration of Scripture, the truthfulness of God, and the consistency he must show in all his acts give us the confidence that nothing in Scripture will be or can be contrary to or contradict what that same Scripture declares to be its center and purpose.

A further difference between fundamentalism and the stance being defended today is seen in the divergent ways in which both think and speak of the matter of inerrancy. Fundamentalists feel threatened by every claimed or apparent error and discrepancy in the sacred text. They write books to explain away difficulties. Whether there was one donkey or two for Jesus to make use of in his entry into Jerusalem before his passion is a matter of critical urgency. Other examples were given in the first lecture. These aspects of the Bible are interesting matters for themselves but are not immediately related to inerrancy, authority, or reliability. I shall let the *Theses of Agreement,* which forms part of the basis of union for the Lutheran Church of Australia, speak on this matter:

> With the whole true Church of God we confess the Bible to be the inerrant Word of God. This inerrancy of the Holy Scriptures cannot be seen with human eyes, nor can it be proved to human reason; it is an article of faith, a belief in something that is hidden and not obvious. We believe that the Scriptures are the Word of God and therefore inerrant. The term 'inerrancy' has no reference to he variant readings found in the extant textual sources because of copyists' errors or deliberate alterations; neither does it imply an absolute verbal accuracy in quotations and in parallel accounts, such absolute uniformity

evidently not having been part of God's design. We believe that the holy writers, whom God used, retained the distinctive features of their personalities (language and terminology, literary methods, conditions of life, knowledge of nature and history as apart from direct revelation and prophecy). God made use of them in such a manner that even that which human reason might call a deficiency in Holy Scripture must serve the divine purpose. Furthermore, it pleased the Holy Ghost to employ authors possessing various gifts for writing on the same subject. How in such cases it is possible that differing accounts of the same event or the same saying are the true and inerrant report of one and the same fact cannot and need not always be shown by rational harmonization.

These words could be misunderstood, as though an endeavor were being made to speak of inerrancy on two different levels, with the level of faith being set beyond the reach of criticism. In 1972 the Lutheran Church of Australia attempted to meet such criticism of the Theses, and this endeavor will be reported in detail below. For the present it is necessary to point out the truth that while proof for the Word is not historically possible, it is historically possible to disprove its assertions. Take the case of the resurrection. No historical proof for this is really possible, for we are not dealing with a strictly historical occurrence like the resuscitation of a corpse, the coming back to this life and mode of existence of one who has died. We are dealing rather with the entry of one who has died into a new and spiritual mode of existence which no other human being has experienced. But disproof of the resurrection is logically thinkable. For instance, if Caiaphas, upon hearing the report from the early Christians that Jesus of Nazareth had risen, had gone to the tomb of Joseph of Arimathea and found there a newly deposited body, he would have had every right to declare that Jesus of Nazareth did not rise. This, by the way, is the importance of the report of the empty tomb in the apostolic witness to the resurrection of Jesus. Inerrancy cannot be proved. It is a matter of faith, not demonstration, as the *Theses of Agreement* declare. But, logically speaking, inerrancy could be disproved if assertion after assertion in the Scriptures could be shown to be mistaken and false. Defense of inerrancy in certain directions is therefore necessary and to the point. Pinnock is basically on the right path when he writes in his book *Biblical Revelation— The Foundation of Christian Theology:*

> Fuller argues that the doctrinal verses teaching inspiration do not require so broad a view, but teach only inerrancy in *revelational matters*. Fuller proposes this as only a "slight corrective" to Warfield, with considerable advantages. It leaves revelational matters (those which for the most part, he claims, lie outside empirical investigation) safe and secure, while difficulties affect only areas where historical control is possible. Here lies the difficulty. The claim that Scripture does *not* err in those places where it may not be tested is meaningless if it *does* err in those places where it can! The extent to which the verifiable portions of Scripture are fallacious is the degree to which the *whole* of Scripture is discredited. Wherever faith and knowledge are opposed like this, faith suffers. The factual assertions of Scripture are bound up with

the theological affirmations (e.g., Matt. 12:
41). The theological truth is discredited to
the extent that the factual material is erroneous.

In basic agreement with this statement the Lutheran Church of Australia in 1972 adopted an
explanatory statement on the matter of inerrancy
as presented in the *Theses of Agreement*. It insisted on the necessity of opposing the idea of
"errors" in the Bible, and at the same time pointed
to inerrancy again as a matter of faith and not of
logical demonstration. Its seven condemnations—
although that term is not used—show particularly
clearly the point that is at present being made.

Some ways of speaking or teaching in the
matter of inerrancy which are contrary to the
sound doctrine of the Scriptures and of the
Theses of Agreement are herewith specified:

1. to speak of "errors" in the Holy Scripture;
2. to hold that what according to clear biblical
   statements "actually is or actually happened" may be regarded as what actually
   is *not* or actually does *not* happen;
3. to adopt uncritically and to propagate all
   the claims of historical criticism which
   often rest on or lead to an unbiblical scep-
   ticism as to the historical bases of the
   Christian faith;
4. to use modern knowledge as a means to
   judge any biblical statement and attack
   the authority of Scripture;
5. to make faith in the inerrancy of Scripture
   in any way depend on the human certainty
   attained by rational argument and demonstration;
6. to regard all statements of the Scripture
   as being of equal value and importance;

> **7.** to treat the Bible in such a way as though
> its divine authority rendered historical in-
> vestigation unimportant or irrelevant.[4]

Sound teaching on inerrancy must do justice to both facts developed in these lectures: (1) The actual state of the biblical texts which readers are presented with, and the claims of the Scripture about itself, which include, of course, the assertions of our Lord and his apostles.

Although the actual texts with which we are confronted do cause difficulties of various kinds, some of them impinging on the subject of inerrancy, at least two observations of importance can be made concerning this class of difficulty. The first is that there are not as many difficulties as is often suggested. A certain class of scholars sees nothing but contradictions of all kinds—they are the counterparts of the rank fundamentalists who see none. When, for instance, an eminent scholar traces the divisions in churches of our day back to the lack of unity of teaching in the biblical writers, he can do this only by magnifying minute variations of theological expression into major differences in the understanding of the gospel. Molehills are made into mountains. Even a modicum of willingness to see harmony where possible between conflicting accounts will remove a considerable number of the traditional and other difficulties that may be encountered.

The second observation is that some of the discrepancies are really of no consequence, and it is only lack of flexibility of mind which would even think that inerrancy is threatened. There are various sayings of Jesus and also a number of stories where the central concern is clear as clear could be, but where there is irreconcilable disagreement way out on the periphery. For example, a famous word of Jesus is transmitted in two quite different ways. Matthew 5:40 reads: "And if any one would sue you and take your coat, let him have your cloak as well." But Luke renders this as follows: "And from him who takes away your coat do not withhold even your shirt" (6:29). To suggest that Jesus spoke the sentence in both ways during his ministry is to be ridiculous. Luke has probably changed the sentence for the benefit of his Gentile readers. But the meaning is precisely the same. There is a formal discrepancy in the actual wording, but complete agreement in what is really said. I hold that inerrancy is not affected by such matters. Similarly, as mentioned earlier, Matthew has two donkeys in the story of Jesus' entry into Jerusalem, while the other evangelists have one. To deny that there ever was an entry of Jesus before his end would indeed be an attack on the inerrancy of the Scripture—clear biblical statements regarding what happened would be made into statements of what did not happen. But the whole episode remains precisely the same no matter how many donkeys were involved. Very many so-called discrepancies can be considered to be such only on a peripheral level.

There are probably gray areas where scholars who are committed to biblical inerrancy differ as to whether a certain position is an attack on inerrancy or not. Some such scholars might be able to live with the view that Second Peter is both pseudonymous and canonical, while others would feel compelled to assert Petrine authorship in some sense or else cease to regard the letter as part of the New Testament. In cases like this, the church must be willing to put up with differences of judgment, putting the best construction upon scholars' opinions or convictions, so long as it is clear from their whole work that they are submissive to the Word of God and the authority of Scripture.

Therefore, if the actual facts of the texts and the biblical claim to inerrancy are kept in proper tension, nothing is lost and much is gained. The biggest gain will be that all can see the church to be honest and truthful, with scholars who are both impelled by convictions of faith and alert to what the Bible actually says as well as refusing to try and make it say what they might like it to say.

The view of the Bible as the Word of God presented here also gives philosophy or human reason its proper place in relation to the Bible. On the negative side, it has already been stated that human reason must be rejected as a source or norm of the Christian religion or its theology. To make the circle of argument complete it is necessary to say something of the positive contribution of human reason to a sound use of the Bible.

Reason is necessary as the means to understand what the Scripture says and to present what it has to say for the understanding of people. God gave his Word (and still gives it through the Scriptures) in human words. The Word of God is written and is spoken in all the logic of human language. Speech is a complicated means of communication. Its logic has been thoroughly investigated in language after language. Most of us know this logic in our mother tongue in a practical way, but a real logic, a real exercise of human reason is going on all the time. So the Bible makes use of the logic of language, and of almost all the kinds of logical argumentation the human mind uses. To understand the Word of God in the Bible and comprehend all the various kinds of literary forms made use of there, human reason and logic are absolutely necessary. All of us, but especially those who teach exegesis and homiletics, know how difficult most people find it to really understand and comprehend a given piece of prose literature or poetry. The same use of human reason is needed to convey the message of the Bible in a clear, understandable, attractive, and interesting way to others, whether by preaching, teaching, or conversation.

A good case could be made, further, for the value of philosophy as a *praeparatio evangelii,* as a preparation for the gospel. Philosophy can serve the negative function of showing how all attempts of the human mind to attain to the final truth about God, life, meaning, and salvation (whether these attempts take the purely logical path, or the ethical, or the mystical) finally lead to the conclusion that the solution is impossible; that the final answer is *ignoramus et ignorabimus,* we don't know and we never shall. We need a revelation from God; we need the God who speaks. In this way, philosophy plays the same role as the law of God in preparing human beings for the message of the gospel.

This use of reason is often described as *ancillary* in order to mark its nature as serving something greater, the Word itself. The use of reason that I have rejected for its part is called the *magisterial* use of reason, a claim that reason is master and has the right to determine what is right and wrong, good and bad, true and false.

I should like to summarize what has been presented by means of various expositions of a well-known biblical passage. The three interpretations more or less characterize the three views of the Bible that have been considered in these chapters. The three interpretations will follow the order of the lectures. So we shall have, first, the fundamentalistic interpretation, then, the one determined by philosophy, and, finally, that which is in accord with what I have argued in these chapters.

The biblical passage I have in mind is that dealing with the Fall, Genesis 3. Fundamentalists normally take the whole story literally. There was a *real* garden, with a *real* snake, *real* trees of life and of the knowledge of good and evil. There was a *real* conversation between a snake (or the devil making use of a snake) and Eve. Not only did Adam and Eve fall grievously into sin, leaving the holy state in which God had created them, but the whole happening took place in precisely the way in which it is described in Genesis.

Now the interpreter who allows philosophy to determine his reading of the story could take the line followed by E. B. Redlich:

> The stories of the Creation and the Fall are also legends explaining the origin of customs and institutions; that is to say, they are aetiological legends. In these two dramatic stories the Hebrews found answers to many questions dealing with human life and interests. When were clothes first worn? Why are serpents hated by man? Why do they crawl along

the ground? Why is man mortal? And in particular, questions relating to sex: What causes sexual attraction? When was marriage instituted? Why is woman subservient to man? Why is birth painful? [5]

A philosophical commentator may take a different line, one that is met with very commonly in theological works. The story in Genesis 3 then becomes a myth or parable of the human situation. Adam and Eve represent all people. The word *Adam* means man, Eve is Hebrew *chayyah*, "life"; she is the mother. The story depicts most truly the root of evil which is in us all. We all, like Adam and Eve, come into temptations which we cannot resist and so fall into sin. Thus there is no history in the event of Genesis 3, no event at the beginning of the human race with catastrophic effects. Professor Alan Richardson puts the case with all possible clarity:

> The time-element in the myths of Creation and Fall (as in all the biblical myths) must be discounted: it is not that *once* (in 4004 B.C.—or a hundred thousand years ago) God created man perfect and then he fell from grace. God is eternally Creator; he is eternally making man and holding him in being and seeing that his handiwork is good (Gen. 1:31). And just as creation is an eternal activity, so the "Fall" is an ingredient of every moment of human life; man is at every moment "falling," putting himself in the centre, rebelling against the will of God. Adam is Everyman. [6]

The third position taken in these lectures would assert the actuality, but would not insist on the literal understanding of the story. So there *was* a Creation and a Fall, not merely continual creating of human beings and continual falling. God *did* create humanity good, as Genesis 1 distinctly states, for nothing that God creates is evil. Evil is *not* part of the created human nature, however certainly it has corrupted that nature. But there *was* a catastrophe in the history of the human race which affected the whole of it. The truth is put in the form of a fictitious tale, but it sets forth actual truth. What is declared to have happened, that the race created good became sinful, truly happened. In setting this forth, the writer made use of material well known to his readers. If he had been writing among the Eskimos, the tale would have looked different, with a polar bear and fish and a forbidden hole in the ice taking the place of the scene we know so well in Genesis. But the happening depicted would still be the same. It can be demonstrated that the text of Genesis 3 itself gives good cause and reason for taking it to be a fictitious tale; like many of the parables of Jesus, its meaning has to be seen underlying the surface presentation.

It should be noted that, with this final interpretation, the underlying truth—the nature and the origin of sin—remains precisely the same as for the fundamentalist. It would be unreasonable and unjust for a fundamentalist to hold that this sort of interpretation of the Fall is in any way an attack on the Bible or its authority. It is an interpretation which actually deals more accurately with the literary form at hand.

Chapter 3 footnotes

1. *The Book of Concord,* Theodore G. Tappert, trans. and ed. (Muhlenberg, 1959), p. 312.
2. Hermann Sasse, Comments on the Report of the Commission on Theology and Church Relations (LCMS), A Study Document on Revelation, Inspiration, Inerrancy, pp. 8-9.
3. *The Book of Concord,* pp. 464-465.
4. Pinnock, p. 79.
5. E. B. Redlich, *The Early Traditions of Genesis* (Duckworth, 1950), pp. 74-75.
6. *A Theological Word Book of the Bible* (Macmillan, 1961), p. 14.